Personal Protective Equipment

U.S. Department of Labor

Occupational Safety and Health Administration

OSHA 3151-12R
2003

Contents

List of Tables

Introduction

Hazards exist in every workplace in many different forms: sharp edges, falling objects, flying sparks, chemicals, noise and a myriad of other potentially dangerous situations. The Occupational Safety and Health Administration (OSHA) requires that employers protect their employees from workplace hazards that can cause injury.

Controlling a hazard at its source is the best way to protect employees. Depending on the hazard or workplace conditions, OSHA recommends the use of engineering or work practice controls to manage or eliminate hazards to the greatest extent possible. For example, building a barrier between the hazard and the employees is an engineering control; changing the way in which employees perform their work is a work practice control.

When engineering, work practice and administrative controls are not feasible or do not provide sufficient protection, employers must provide personal protective equipment (PPE) to their employees and ensure its use. Personal protective equipment, commonly referred to as "PPE", is equipment worn to minimize exposure to a variety of hazards. Examples of PPE include such items as gloves, foot and eye protection, protective hearing devices (earplugs, muffs) hard hats, respirators and full body suits.

This guide will help both employers and employees do the following:

- Understand the types of PPE.

- Know the basics of conducting a "hazard assessment" of the workplace.

- Select appropriate PPE for a variety of circumstances.

- Understand what kind of training is needed in the proper use and care of PPE.

The information in this guide is general in nature and does not address all workplace hazards or PPE requirements. The information, methods and procedures in this guide are based on the OSHA requirements for PPE as set forth in the Code of Federal Regulations (CFR) at 29 CFR 1910.132 (General requirements); 29 CFR 1910.133 (Eye and face protection); 29 CFR 1910.135 (Head protection); 29 CFR 1910.136 (Foot protection); 29 CFR 1910. 137 (Electrical protective equipment); 29 CFR 1910.138 (Hand protection); and regulations that cover the construction industry, at

29 CFR 1926.95 (Criteria for personal protective equipment); 29 CFR 1926.96 (Occupational foot protection); 29 CFR 1926.100 (Head protection); 29 CFR 1926.101 (Hearing protection); and 29 CFR 1926.102 (Eye and face protection); and for the maritime industry at 29 CFR 1915.152 (General requirements); 29 CFR 1915.153 (Eye and face protection); 29 CFR 1915.155 (Head protection); 29 CFR 1915.156 (Foot protection); and 29 CFR 1915.157 (Hand and body protection).

This guide does not address PPE requirements related to respiratory protection (29 CFR 1910.134) as this information is covered in detail in OSHA Publication 3079, "Respiratory Protection". There is a brief discussion of hearing protection in this publication but users should refer to OSHA Publication 3074, "Hearing Conservation" for more detailed information on the requirements to protect employees' hearing in the workplace.

The Requirement for PPE

To ensure the greatest possible protection for employees in the workplace, the cooperative efforts of both employers and employees will help in establishing and maintaining a safe and healthful work environment.

In general, employers are responsible for:

- Performing a "hazard assessment" of the workplace to identify and control physical and health hazards.
- Identifying and providing appropriate PPE for employees.
- Training employees in the use and care of the PPE.
- Maintaining PPE, including replacing worn or damaged PPE.
- Periodically reviewing, updating and evaluating the effectiveness of the PPE program.

In general, employees should:

- Properly wear PPE,
- Attend training sessions on PPE,
- Care for, clean and maintain PPE, and
- Inform a supervisor of the need to repair or replace PPE.

Specific requirements for PPE are presented in many different OSHA standards, published in 29 CFR. Some standards require that employers provide PPE at no cost to the employee while others simply state that the employer must provide PPE. Appendix A at page 40 lists those standards that require the employer to provide PPE and those that require the employer to provide PPE at no cost to the employee.

The Hazard Assessment

A first critical step in developing a comprehensive safety and health program is to identify physical and health hazards in the workplace. This process is known as a "hazard assessment." Potential hazards may be physical or health-related and a comprehensive hazard assessment should identify hazards in both categories. Examples of physical hazards include moving objects, fluctuating temperatures, high intensity lighting, rolling or pinching objects, electrical connections and sharp edges. Examples of health hazards include overexposure to harmful dusts, chemicals or radiation.

The hazard assessment should begin with a walk-through survey of the facility to develop a list of potential hazards in the following basic hazard categories:

- Impact,
- Penetration,
- Compression (roll-over),
- Chemical,
- Heat/cold,
- Harmful dust,
- Light (optical) radiation, and
- Biologic.

In addition to noting the basic layout of the facility and reviewing any history of occupational illnesses or injuries, things to look for during the walk-through survey include:

- Sources of electricity.
- Sources of motion such as machines or processes where

movement may exist that could result in an impact between personnel and equipment.

- Sources of high temperatures that could result in burns, eye injuries or fire.
- Types of chemicals used in the workplace.
- Sources of harmful dusts.
- Sources of light radiation, such as welding, brazing, cutting, furnaces, heat treating, high intensity lights, etc.
- The potential for falling or dropping objects.
- Sharp objects that could poke, cut, stab or puncture.
- Biologic hazards such as blood or other potentially infected material.

When the walk-through is complete, the employer should organize and analyze the data so that it may be efficiently used in determining the proper types of PPE required at the worksite. The employer should become aware of the different types of PPE available and the levels of protection offered. It is definitely a good idea to select PPE that will provide a level of protection greater than the minimum required to protect employees from hazards.

The workplace should be periodically reassessed for any changes in conditions, equipment or operating procedures that could affect occupational hazards. This periodic reassessment should also include a review of injury and illness records to spot any trends or areas of concern and taking appropriate corrective action. The suitability of existing PPE, including an evaluation of its condition and age, should be included in the reassessment.

Documentation of the hazard assessment is required through a written certification that includes the following information:

- Identification of the workplace evaluated;
- Name of the person conducting the assessment;
- Date of the assessment; and
- Identification of the document certifying completion of the hazard assessment.

Selecting PPE

All PPE clothing and equipment should be of safe design and construction, and should be maintained in a clean and reliable fashion. Employers should take the fit and comfort of PPE into consideration when selecting appropriate items for their workplace. PPE that fits well and is comfortable to wear will encourage employee use of PPE. Most protective devices are available in multiple sizes and care should be taken to select the proper size for each employee. If several different types of PPE are worn together, make sure they are compatible. If PPE does not fit properly, it can make the difference between being safely covered or dangerously exposed. It may not provide the level of protection desired and may discourage employee use.

OSHA requires that many categories of PPE meet or be equivalent to standards developed by the American National Standards Institute (ANSI). ANSI has been preparing safety standards since the 1920s, when the first safety standard was approved to protect the heads and eyes of industrial workers. Employers who need to provide PPE in the categories listed below must make certain that any new equipment procured meets the cited ANSI standard. Existing PPE stocks must meet the ANSI standard in effect at the time of its manufacture or provide protection equivalent to PPE manufactured to the ANSI criteria. Employers should inform employees who provide their own PPE of the employer's selection decisions and ensure that any employee-owned PPE used in the workplace conforms to the employer's criteria, based on the hazard assessment, OSHA requirements and ANSI standards. OSHA requires PPE to meet the following ANSI standards:

- Eye and Face Protection: ANSI Z87.1-1989 (USA Standard for Occupational and Educational Eye and Face Protection).

- Head Protection: ANSI Z89.1-1986.

- Foot Protection: ANSI Z41.1-1991.

For hand protection, there is no ANSI standard for gloves but OSHA recommends that selection be based upon the tasks to be performed and the performance and construction characteristics of the glove material. For protection against chemicals, glove selection must be based on the chemicals encountered, the chemical resistance and the physical properties of the glove material.

Training Employees in the Proper Use of PPE

Employers are required to train each employee who must use PPE. Employees must be trained to know at least the following:

- When PPE is necessary.
- What PPE is necessary.
- How to properly put on, take off, adjust and wear the PPE.
- The limitations of the PPE.
- Proper care, maintenance, useful life and disposal of PPE.

Employers should make sure that each employee demonstrates an understanding of the PPE training as well as the ability to properly wear and use PPE before they are allowed to perform work requiring the use of the PPE. If an employer believes that a previously trained employee is not demonstrating the proper understanding and skill level in the use of PPE, that employee should receive retraining. Other situations that require additional or retraining of employees include the following circumstances: changes in the workplace or in the type of required PPE that make prior training obsolete.

The employer must document the training of each employee required to wear or use PPE by preparing a certification containing the name of each employee trained, the date of training and a clear identification of the subject of the certification.

Eye and Face Protection

Employees can be exposed to a large number of hazards that pose danger to their eyes and face. OSHA requires employers to ensure that employees have appropriate eye or face protection if they are exposed to eye or face hazards from flying particles, molten metal, liquid chemicals, acids or caustic liquids, chemical gases or vapors, potentially infected material or potentially harmful light radiation.

Many occupational eye injuries occur because workers are not wearing any eye protection while others result from wearing improper or poorly fitting eye protection. Employers must be sure that their employees wear appropriate eye and face protection and that the selected form of protection is appropriate to the work being performed and properly fits each worker exposed to the hazard.

Prescription Lenses

Everyday use of prescription corrective lenses will not provide adequate protection against most occupational eye and face hazards, so employers must make sure that employees with corrective lenses either wear eye protection that incorporates the prescription into the design or wear additional eye protection over their prescription lenses. It is important to ensure that the protective eyewear does not disturb the proper positioning of the prescription lenses so that the employee's vision will not be inhibited or limited. Also, employees who wear contact lenses must wear eye or face PPE when working in hazardous conditions.

Eye Protection for Exposed Workers

OSHA suggests that eye protection be routinely considered for use by carpenters, electricians, machinists, mechanics, millwrights, plumbers and pipefitters, sheetmetal workers and tinsmiths, assemblers, sanders, grinding machine operators, sawyers, welders, laborers, chemical process operators and handlers, and timber cutting and logging workers. Employers of workers in other job categories should decide whether there is a need for eye and face PPE through a hazard assessment.

Examples of potential eye or face injuries include:

- Dust, dirt, metal or wood chips entering the eye from activities such as chipping, grinding, sawing, hammering, the use of power tools or even strong wind forces.

- Chemical splashes from corrosive substances, hot liquids, solvents or other hazardous solutions.

- Objects swinging into the eye or face, such as tree limbs, chains, tools or ropes.

- Radiant energy from welding, harmful rays from the use of lasers or other radiant light (as well as heat, glare, sparks, splash and flying particles).

Types of Eye Protection

Selecting the most suitable eye and face protection for employees should take into consideration the following elements:

- Ability to protect against specific workplace hazards.

- Should fit properly and be reasonably comfortable to wear.

- Should provide unrestricted vision and movement.

- Should be durable and cleanable.

- Should allow unrestricted functioning of any other required PPE.

The eye and face protection selected for employee use must clearly identify the manufacturer. Any new eye and face protective devices must comply with ANSI Z87.1-1989 or be at least as effective as this standard requires. Any equipment purchased before this requirement took effect on July 5, 1994, must comply with the earlier ANSI Standard (ANSI Z87.1-1968) or be shown to be equally effective.

An employer may choose to provide one pair of protective eyewear for each position rather than individual eyewear for each employee. If this is done, the employer must make sure that employees disinfect shared protective eyewear after each use. Protective eyewear with corrective lenses may only be used by the employee for whom the corrective prescription was issued and may not be shared among employees.

Some of the most common types of eye and face protection include the following:

- **Safety spectacles**. These protective eyeglasses have safety frames constructed of metal or plastic and impact-resistant lenses. Side shields are available on some models.

- **Goggles**. These are tight-fitting eye protection that completely cover the eyes, eye sockets and the facial area immediately surrounding the eyes and provide protection from impact, dust and splashes. Some goggles will fit over corrective lenses.

- **Welding shields**. Constructed of vulcanized fiber or fiberglass and fitted with a filtered lens, welding shields protect eyes from burns caused by infrared or intense radiant light; they also protect both the eyes and face from flying sparks, metal spatter and slag chips produced during welding, brazing, soldering and cutting operations. OSHA requires filter lenses to have a shade number appropriate to protect against the specific hazards of the work being performed in order to protect against harmful light radiation.

▪ **Laser safety goggles.** These specialty goggles protect against intense concentrations of light produced by lasers. The type of laser safety goggles an employer chooses will depend upon the equipment and operating conditions in the workplace.

▪ **Face shields.** These transparent sheets of plastic extend from the eyebrows to below the chin and across the entire width of the employee's head. Some are polarized for glare protection. Face shields protect against nuisance dusts and potential splashes or sprays of hazardous liquids but will not provide adequate protection against impact hazards. Face shields used in combination with goggles or safety spectacles will provide additional protection against impact hazards.

Each type of protective eyewear is designed to protect against specific hazards. Employers can identify the specific workplace hazards that threaten employees' eyes and faces by completing a hazard assessment as outlined in the earlier section.

Welding Operations

The intense light associated with welding operations can cause serious and sometimes permanent eye damage if operators do not wear proper eye protection. The intensity of light or radiant energy produced by welding, cutting or brazing operations varies according to a number of factors including the task producing the light, the electrode size and the arc current. The following table shows the minimum protective shades for a variety of welding, cutting and brazing operations in general industry and in the shipbuilding industry.

Table 1
Filter Lenses for Protection Against Radiant Energy

Operations	Electrode size in 1/32" (0.8mm)	Arc current	Minimum* protective shade
Shielded metal arc welding	< 3	< 60	7
	3 - 5	60 - 160	8
	5 - 8	160 - 250	10
	> 8	250 - 550	11
Gas metal arc welding and flux cored arc welding		< 60	7
		60 - 160	10
		160 - 250	10
		250 - 500	10
Gas tungsten arc welding		< 50	8
		50 - 150	8
		150 - 500	10
Air carbon	(light)	< 500	10
Arc cutting	(heavy)	500 - 1,000	11
Plasma arc welding		< 20	6
		20 - 100	8
		100 - 400	10
		400 - 800	11
Plasma arc cutting	(light)**	< 300	8
	(medium)**	300 - 400	9
	(heavy)**	400 - 800	10
Torch brazing			3
Torch soldering			2
Carbon arc welding			14

Table 1 (continued)
Filter Lenses for Protection Against Radiant Energy

Operations	Plate thickness inches	Plate thickness mm	Minimum* protective shade
Gas welding: Light	< 1/8	< 3.2	4
Gas welding: Medium	1/8 - 1/2	3.2 - 12.7	5
Gas welding: Heavy	> 1/2	> 12.7	6
Oxygen cutting: Light	< 1	< 25	3
Oxygen cutting: Medium	1 - 6	25 - 150	4
Oxygen cutting: Heavy	> 6	> 150	5

Source: 29 CFR 1910.133(a)(5).

* As a rule of thumb, start with a shade that is too dark to see the weld zone. Then go to a lighter shade which gives sufficient view of the weld zone without going below the minimum. In oxyfuel gas welding or cutting where the torch produces a high yellow light, it is desirable to use a filter lens that absorbs the yellow or sodium line in the visible light of the (spectrum) operation.

**These values apply where the actual arc is clearly seen. Experience has shown that lighter filters may be used when the arc is hidden by the workpiece.

The construction industry has separate requirements for filter lens protective levels for specific types of welding operations, as indicated in the table below:

Table 2
Construction Industry Requirements for Filter Lens Shade Numbers for Protection Against Radiant Energy

Welding Operation	Shade Number
Shielded metal-arc welding 1/16-, 3/32-, 1/8-, 5/32-inch diameter electrodes	10
Gas-shielded arc welding (nonferrous) 1/16-, 3/32-, 1/8-, 5/32-inch diameter electrodes	11
Gas-shielded arc welding (ferrous) 1/16-, 3/32-, 1/8-, 5/32-inch diameter electrodes	12
Shielded metal-arc welding 3/16-, 7/32-, 1/4-inch diameter electrodes	12
5/16-, 3/8-inch diameter electrodes	14
Atomic hydrogen welding	10 - 14
Carbon-arc welding	14
Soldering	2
Torch brazing	3 or 4
Light cutting, up to 1 inch	3 or 4
Medium cutting, 1 to 6 inches	4 or 5
Heavy cutting, more than 6 inches	5 or 6
Gas welding (light), up to 1/8-inch	4 or 5
Gas welding (medium), 1/8- to 1/2-inch	5 or 6
Gas welding (heavy), more than 1/2-inch	6 or 8

Source: 29 CFR 1926.102(b)(1).

Laser light radiation can be extremely dangerous to the unprotected eye and direct or reflected beams can cause permanent eye damage. Laser retinal burns can be painless, so it is essential that all personnel in or around laser operations wear appropriate eye protection.

Laser safety goggles should protect for the specific wavelength of the laser and must be of sufficient optical density for the energy involved. Safety goggles intended for use with laser beams must be labeled with the laser wavelengths for which they are intended to be used, the optical density of those wavelengths and the visible light transmission.

The table below lists maximum power or energy densities and appropriate protection levels for optical densities 5 through 8.

Table 3
Selecting Laser Safety Glass

Intensity, CW maximum power density (watts/cm²)	Attenuation	
	Optical density (O.D.)	Attenuation factor
10^{-2}	5	10^5
10^{-1}	6	10^6
1.0	7	10^7
10.0	8	10^8

Source: 29 CFR 1926.102(b)(2).

Head Protection

Protecting employees from potential head injuries is a key element of any safety program. A head injury can impair an employee for life or it can be fatal. Wearing a safety helmet or hard hat is one of the easiest ways to protect an employee's head from injury. Hard hats can protect employees from impact and penetration hazards as well as from electrical shock and burn hazards.

Employers must ensure that their employees wear head protection if any of the following apply:

- Objects might fall from above and strike them on the head;
- They might bump their heads against fixed objects, such as exposed pipes or beams; or
- There is a possibility of accidental head contact with electrical hazards.

Some examples of occupations in which employees should be required to wear head protection include construction workers, carpenters, electricians, linemen, plumbers and pipefitters, timber and log cutters, welders, among many others. Whenever there is a danger of objects falling from above, such as working below others who are using tools or working under a conveyor belt, head protection must be worn. Hard hats must be worn with the bill forward to protect employees properly.

In general, protective helmets or hard hats should do the following:

- Resist penetration by objects.
- Absorb the shock of a blow.
- Be water-resistant and slow burning.
- Have clear instructions explaining proper adjustment and replacement of the suspension and headband.

Hard hats must have a hard outer shell and a shock-absorbing lining that incorporates a headband and straps that suspend the shell from 1 to 1 1/4 inches (2.54 cm to 3.18 cm) away from the head. This type of design provides shock absorption during an impact and ventilation during normal wear.

Protective headgear must meet ANSI Standard Z89.1-1986 (Protective Headgear for Industrial Workers) or provide an equivalent level of protection. Helmets purchased before July 5, 1994 must comply with the earlier ANSI Standard (Z89.1-1969) or provide equivalent protection.

Types of Hard Hats

There are many types of hard hats available in the marketplace today. In addition to selecting protective headgear that meets ANSI standard requirements, employers should ensure that employees wear hard hats that provide appropriate protection against potential workplace hazards. It is important for employers to understand all potential hazards when making this selection, including electrical hazards. This can be done through a comprehensive hazard analysis and an awareness of the different types of protective headgear available.

Hard hats are divided into three industrial classes:

- **Class A hard hats** provide impact and penetration resistance along with limited voltage protection (up to 2,200 volts).

- **Class B hard hats** provide the highest level of protection against electrical hazards, with high-voltage shock and burn protection (up to 20,000 volts). They also provide protection from impact and penetration hazards by flying/falling objects.

- **Class C hard hats** provide lightweight comfort and impact protection but offer no protection from electrical hazards.

Another class of protective headgear on the market is called a "bump hat," designed for use in areas with low head clearance. They are recommended for areas where protection is needed from head bumps and lacerations. These are not designed to protect against falling or flying objects and are not ANSI approved. It is essential to check the type of hard hat employees are using to ensure that the equipment provides appropriate protection. Each hat should bear a label inside the shell that lists the manufacturer, the ANSI designation and the class of the hat.

Size and Care Considerations

Head protection that is either too large or too small is inappropriate for use, even if it meets all other requirements. Protective headgear must fit appropriately on the body and for the head size of each individual. Most protective headgear comes in a variety of sizes with adjustable headbands to ensure a proper fit (many adjust in 1/8-inch increments). A proper fit should allow sufficient clearance between the shell and the suspension system for ventilation and distribution of an impact. The hat should not bind, slip, fall off or irritate the skin.

Some protective headgear allows for the use of various accessories to help employees deal with changing environmental conditions, such as slots for earmuffs, safety glasses, face shields and mounted lights. Optional brims may provide additional protection from the sun and some hats have channels that guide rainwater away from the face. Protective headgear accessories must not compromise the safety elements of the equipment.

Periodic cleaning and inspection will extend the useful life of protective headgear. A daily inspection of the hard hat shell, suspension system and other accessories for holes, cracks, tears or other damage that might compromise the protective value of the hat is essential. Paints, paint thinners and some cleaning agents can weaken the shells of hard hats and may eliminate electrical resistance. Consult the helmet manufacturer for information on the effects of paint and cleaning materials on their hard hats. Never drill holes, paint or apply labels to protective headgear as this may reduce the integrity of the protection. Do not store protective headgear in direct sunlight, such as on the rear window shelf of a car, since sunlight and extreme heat can damage them.

Hard hats with any of the following defects should be removed from service and replaced:

▪ Perforation, cracking, or deformity of the brim or shell;

▪ Indication of exposure of the brim or shell to heat, chemicals or ultraviolet light and other radiation (in addition to a loss of surface gloss, such signs include chalking or flaking).

Always replace a hard hat if it sustains an impact, even if damage is not noticeable. Suspension systems are offered as replacement parts and should be replaced when damaged or when excessive wear is noticed. It is not necessary to replace the entire hard hat when deterioration or tears of the suspension systems are noticed.

Foot and Leg Protection

Employees who face possible foot or leg injuries from falling or rolling objects or from crushing or penetrating materials should wear protective footwear. Also, employees whose work involves exposure to hot substances or corrosive or poisonous materials must have protective gear to cover exposed body parts, including legs and feet. If an employee's feet may be exposed to electrical hazards, non-conductive footwear should be worn. On the other hand, workplace exposure to static electricity may necessitate the use of conductive footwear.

Examples of situations in which an employee should wear foot and/or leg protection include:

- When heavy objects such as barrels or tools might roll onto or fall on the employee's feet;

- Working with sharp objects such as nails or spikes that could pierce the soles or uppers of ordinary shoes;

- Exposure to molten metal that might splash on feet or legs;

- Working on or around hot, wet or slippery surfaces; and

- Working when electrical hazards are present.

Safety footwear must meet ANSI minimum compression and impact performance standards in ANSI Z41-1991 (American National Standard for Personal Protection-Protective Footwear) or provide equivalent protection. Footwear purchased before July 5, 1994, must meet or provide equivalent protection to the earlier ANSI Standard (ANSI Z41.1-1967). All ANSI approved footwear has a protective toe and offers impact and compression protection. But the type and amount of protection is not always the same. Different footwear protects in different ways. Check the product's labeling or consult the manufacturer to make sure the footwear will protect the user from the hazards they face.

Foot and leg protection choices include the following:

- **Leggings** protect the lower legs and feet from heat hazards such as molten metal or welding sparks. Safety snaps allow leggings to be removed quickly.

- **Metatarsal guards** protect the instep area from impact and compression. Made of aluminum, steel, fiber or plastic, these guards may be strapped to the outside of shoes.

- **Toe guards** fit over the toes of regular shoes to protect the toes from impact and compression hazards. They may be made of steel, aluminum or plastic.

- **Combination foot and shin guards** protect the lower legs and feet, and may be used in combination with toe guards when greater protection is needed.

- **Safety shoes** have impact-resistant toes and heat-resistant soles that protect the feet against hot work surfaces common in roofing, paving and hot metal industries. The metal insoles of some safety shoes protect against puncture wounds. Safety shoes may also be designed to be electrically conductive to prevent the buildup of static electricity in areas with the potential for explosive atmospheres or nonconductive to protect workers from workplace electrical hazards.

Special Purpose Shoes

Electrically conductive shoes provide protection against the buildup of static electricity. Employees working in explosive and hazardous locations such as explosives manufacturing facilities or grain elevators must wear conductive shoes to reduce the risk of static electricity buildup on the body that could produce a spark and cause an explosion or fire. Foot powder should not be used in conjunction with protective conductive footwear because it provides insulation, reducing the conductive ability of the shoes. Silk, wool and nylon socks can produce static electricity and should not be worn with conductive footwear. Conductive shoes must be removed when the task requiring their use is completed. Note: Employees exposed to electrical hazards must never wear conductive shoes.

Electrical hazard, safety-toe shoes are nonconductive and will prevent the wearers' feet from completing an electrical circuit to the ground. These shoes can protect against open circuits of up to 600 volts in dry conditions and should be used in conjunction with other insulating equipment and additional precautions to reduce the risk of a worker becoming a path for hazardous electrical energy. The insulating protection of electrical hazard, safety-toe shoes may be compromised if the shoes become wet, the soles are worn through, metal particles become embedded in the sole or heel, or workers touch conductive, grounded items. Note: Nonconductive footwear must not be used in explosive or hazardous locations.

Foundry Shoes

In addition to insulating the feet from the extreme heat of molten metal, foundry shoes keep hot metal from lodging in shoe eyelets, tongues or other shoe parts. These snug-fitting leather or leather-substitute shoes have leather or rubber soles and rubber heels. All foundry shoes must have built-in safety toes.

Care of Protective Footwear

As with all protective equipment, safety footwear should be inspected prior to each use. Shoes and leggings should be checked for wear and tear at reasonable intervals. This includes looking for cracks or holes, separation of materials, broken buckles or laces. The soles of shoes should be checked for pieces of metal or other embedded items that could present electrical or tripping hazards. Employees should follow the manufacturers' recommendations for cleaning and maintenance of protective footwear.

Hand and Arm Protection

If a workplace hazard assessment reveals that employees face potential injury to hands and arms that cannot be eliminated through engineering and work practice controls, employers must ensure that employees wear appropriate protection. Potential hazards include skin absorption of harmful substances, chemical or thermal burns, electrical dangers, bruises, abrasions, cuts, punctures, fractures and amputations. Protective equipment includes gloves, finger guards and arm coverings or elbow-length gloves.

Employers should explore all possible engineering and work practice controls to eliminate hazards and use PPE to provide additional protection against hazards that cannot be completely eliminated through other means. For example, machine guards may eliminate a hazard. Installing a barrier to prevent workers from placing their hands at the point of contact between a table saw blade and the item being cut is another method.

Types of Protective Gloves

There are many types of gloves available today to protect against a wide variety of hazards. The nature of the hazard and the operation involved will affect the selection of gloves. The variety of potential occupational hand injuries makes selecting the right pair of gloves challenging. It is essential that employees use gloves specifically designed for the hazards and tasks found in their workplace because gloves designed for one function may not protect against a different function even though they may appear to be an appropriate protective device.

The following are examples of some factors that may influence the selection of protective gloves for a workplace.

- Type of chemicals handled.

- Nature of contact (total immersion, splash, etc.).

- Duration of contact.

- Area requiring protection (hand only, forearm, arm).

- Grip requirements (dry, wet, oily).

- Thermal protection.

- Size and comfort.

- Abrasion/resistance requirements.

Gloves made from a wide variety of materials are designed for many types of workplace hazards. In general, gloves fall into four groups:

- Gloves made of leather, canvas or metal mesh;

- Fabric and coated fabric gloves;

- Chemical- and liquid-resistant gloves;

- Insulating rubber gloves (See 29 CFR 1910.137 and the following section on electrical protective equipment for detailed requirements on the selection, use and care of insulating rubber gloves).

Leather, Canvas or Metal Mesh Gloves

Sturdy gloves made from metal mesh, leather or canvas provide protection against cuts and burns. Leather or canvass gloves also protect against sustained heat.

- **Leather gloves** protect against sparks, moderate heat, blows, chips and rough objects.

- **Aluminized gloves** provide reflective and insulating protection against heat and require an insert made of synthetic materials to protect against heat and cold.

- **Aramid fiber gloves** protect against heat and cold, are cut- and abrasive-resistant and wear well.

- **Synthetic gloves** of various materials offer protection against heat and cold, are cut- and abrasive-resistant and may withstand some diluted acids. These materials do not stand up against alkalis and solvents.

Fabric and Coated Fabric Gloves

Fabric and coated fabric gloves are made of cotton or other fabric to provide varying degrees of protection.

- **Fabric gloves** protect against dirt, slivers, chafing and abrasions. They do not provide sufficient protection for use with rough, sharp or heavy materials. Adding a plastic coating will strengthen some fabric gloves.

- **Coated fabric gloves** are normally made from cotton flannel with napping on one side. By coating the unnapped side with plastic, fabric gloves are transformed into general-purpose hand protection offering slip-resistant qualities. These gloves are used for tasks ranging from handling bricks and wire to chemical laboratory containers. When selecting gloves to protect against chemical exposure hazards, always check with the manufacturer or review the manufacturer's product literature to determine the gloves' effectiveness against specific workplace chemicals and conditions.

Chemical- and Liquid-Resistant Gloves

Chemical-resistant gloves are made with different kinds of rubber: natural, butyl, neoprene, nitrile and fluorocarbon (viton); or various kinds of plastic: polyvinyl chloride (PVC), polyvinyl alcohol and polyethylene. These materials can be blended or laminated for better performance. As a general rule, the thicker the glove material, the greater the chemical resistance but thick gloves may impair grip and dexterity, having a negative impact on safety.

Some examples of chemical-resistant gloves include:

- **Butyl gloves** are made of a synthetic rubber and protect against a wide variety of chemicals, such as peroxide, rocket fuels, highly corrosive acids (nitric acid, sulfuric acid, hydrofluoric acid and red-fuming nitric acid), strong bases, alcohols, aldehydes, ketones, esters and nitrocompounds. Butyl gloves also resist oxidation, ozone corrosion and abrasion, and remain flexible at low temperatures. Butyl rubber does not perform well with aliphatic and aromatic hydrocarbons and halogenated solvents.

- **Natural (latex) rubber gloves** are comfortable to wear, which makes them a popular general-purpose glove. They feature outstanding tensile strength, elasticity and temperature resistance. In addition to resisting abrasions caused by grinding and polishing, these gloves protect workers' hands from most water solutions of acids, alkalis, salts and ketones. Latex gloves have caused allergic reactions in some individuals and may not be appropriate for all employees. Hypoallergenic gloves, glove liners and powderless gloves are possible alternatives for workers who are allergic to latex gloves.

- **Neoprene gloves** are made of synthetic rubber and offer good pliability, finger dexterity, high density and tear resistance. They protect against hydraulic fluids, gasoline, alcohols, organic acids and alkalis. They generally have chemical and wear resistance properties superior to those made of natural rubber.

- **Nitrile gloves** are made of a copolymer and provide protection from chlorinated solvents such as trichloroethylene and per-chloroethylene. Although intended for jobs requiring dexterity and sensitivity, nitrile gloves stand up to heavy use even after prolonged exposure to substances that cause other gloves to deteriorate. They offer protection when working with oils, greases, acids, caustics and alcohols but are generally not recommended for use with strong oxidizing agents, aromatic solvents, ketones and acetates.

The following table from the U.S. Department of Energy (Occupational Safety and Health Technical Reference Manual) rates various gloves as being protective against specific chemicals and will help you select the most appropriate gloves to protect your employees. The ratings are abbreviated as follows: VG: Very Good; G: Good; F: Fair; P: Poor (not recommended). Chemicals marked with an asterisk (*) are for limited service.

Table 4
Chemical Resistance Selection Chart for Protective Gloves

Chemical	Neoprene	Latex/Rubber	Butyl	Nitrile
Acetaldehyde*	VG	G	VG	G
Acetic acid	VG	VG	VG	VG
Acetone*	G	VG	VG	P
Ammonium hydroxide	VG	VG	VG	VG
Amy acetate*	F	P	F	P
Aniline	G	F	F	P
Benzaldehyde*	F	F	G	G
Benzene*	P	P	P	F
Butyl acetate	G	F	F	P
Butyl alcohol	VG	VG	VG	VG
Carbon disulfide	F	F	F	F
Carbon tetrachloride*	F	P	P	G
Castor oil	F	P	F	VG
Chlorobenzene*	F	P	F	P
Chloroform*	G	P	P	F
Chloronaphthalene	F	P	F	F
Chromic acid (50%)	F	P	F	F
Citric acid (10%)	VG	VG	VG	VG
Cyclohexanol	G	F	G	VG
Dibutyl phthalate*	G	P	G	G
Diesel fuel	G	P	P	VG
Diisobutyl ketone	P	F	G	P
Dimethylformamide	F	F	G	G
Dioctyl phthalate	G	P	F	VG
Dioxane	VG	G	G	G

Epoxy resins, dry	VG	VG	VG	VG
Ethyl acetate*	G	F	G	F
Ethyl alcohol	VG	VG	VG	VG
Ethyl ether*	VG	G	VG	G
Ethylene dichloride*	F	P	F	P
Ethylene glycol	VG	VG	VG	VG
Formaldehyde	VG	VG	VG	VG
Formic acid	VG	VG	VG	VG
Freon 11	G	P	F	G
Freon 12	G	P	F	G
Freon 21	G	P	F	G
Freon 22	G	P	F	G
Furfural*	G	G	G	G
Gasoline, leaded	G	P	F	VG
Gasoline, unleaded	G	P	F	VG
Glycerin	VG	VG	VG	VG
Hexane	F	P	P	G
Hydrazine (65%)	F	G	G	G
Hydrochloric acid	VG	G	G	G
Hydrofluoric acid (48%)	VG	G	G	G
Hydrogen peroxide (30%)	G	G	G	G
Hydroquinone	G	G	G	F
Isooctane	F	P	P	VG
Kerosene	VG	F	F	VG
Ketones	G	VG	VG	P
Lacquer thinners	G	F	F	P
Lactic acid (85%)	VG	VG	VG	VG
Lauric acid (36%)	VG	F	VG	VG
Lineolic acid	VG	P	F	G
Linseed oil	VG	P	F	VG
Maleic acid	VG	VG	VG	VG
Methyl alcohol	VG	VG	VG	VG
Methylamine	F	F	G	G
Methyl bromide	G	F	G	F
Methyl chloride*	P	P	P	P

Methyl ethyl ketone*	G	G	VG	P
Methyl isobutyl ketone*	F	F	VG	P
Methyl metharcrylate	G	G	VG	F
Monoethanolamine	VG	G	VG	VG
Morpholine	VG	VG	VG	G
Naphthalene	G	F	F	G
Napthas, aliphatic	VG	F	F	VG
Napthas, aromatic	G	P	P	G
Nitric acid*	G	F	F	F
Nitric acid, red and white fuming	P	P	P	P
Nitromethane (95.5%)*	F	P	F	F
Nitropropane (95.5%)	F	P	F	F
Octyl alcohol	VG	VG	VG	VG
Oleic acid	VG	F	G	VG
Oxalic acid	VG	VG	VG	VG
Palmitic acid	VG	VG	VG	VG
Perchloric acid (60%)	VG	F	G	G
Perchloroethylene	F	P	P	G
Petroleum distillates (naphtha)	G	P	P	VG
Phenol	VG	F	G	F
Phosphoric acid	VG	G	VG	VG
Potassium hydroxide	VG	VG	VG	VG
Propyl acetate	G	F	G	F
Propyl alcohol	VG	VG	VG	VG
Propyl alcohol (iso)	VG	VG	VG	VG
Sodium hydroxide	VG	VG	VG	VG
Styrene	P	P	P	F
Styrene (100%)	P	P	P	F
Sulfuric acid	G	G	G	G
Tannic acid (65)	VG	VG	VG	VG
Tetrahydrofuran	P	F	F	F
Toluene*	F	P	P	F
Toluene diisocyanate (TDI)	F	G	G	F

Table 4 (continued) Chemical Resistance Selection Chart for Protective Gloves				
Trichloroethylene*	F	F	P	G
Triethanolamine (85%)	VG	G	G	VG
Tung oil	VG	P	F	VG
Turpentine	G	F	F	VG
Xylene*	P	P	P	F

Note: When selecting chemical-resistant gloves be sure to consult the manufacturer's recommendations, especially if the gloved hand(s) will be immersed in the chemical.

Care of Protective Gloves

Protective gloves should be inspected before each use to ensure that they are not torn, punctured or made ineffective in any way. A visual inspection will help detect cuts or tears but a more thorough inspection by filling the gloves with water and tightly rolling the cuff towards the fingers will help reveal any pinhole leaks. Gloves that are discolored or stiff may also indicate deficiencies caused by excessive use or degradation from chemical exposure.

Any gloves with impaired protective ability should be discarded and replaced. Reuse of chemical-resistant gloves should be evaluated carefully, taking into consideration the absorptive qualities of the gloves. A decision to reuse chemically-exposed gloves should take into consideration the toxicity of the chemicals involved and factors such as duration of exposure, storage and temperature.

Body Protection

Employees who face possible bodily injury of any kind that cannot be eliminated through engineering, work practice or administrative controls, must wear appropriate body protection while performing their jobs. In addition to cuts and radiation, the following are examples of workplace hazards that could cause bodily injury:

- Temperature extremes;

- Hot splashes from molten metals and other hot liquids;

- Potential impacts from tools, machinery and materials;
- Hazardous chemicals.

There are many varieties of protective clothing available for specific hazards. Employers are required to ensure that their employees wear personal protective equipment only for the parts of the body exposed to possible injury. Examples of body protection include laboratory coats, coveralls, vests, jackets, aprons, surgical gowns and full body suits.

If a hazard assessment indicates a need for full body protection against toxic substances or harmful physical agents, the clothing should be carefully inspected before each use, it must fit each worker properly and it must function properly and for the purpose for which it is intended.

Protective clothing comes in a variety of materials, each effective against particular hazards, such as:

- **Paper-like fiber** used for disposable suits provide protection against dust and splashes.

- **Treated wool and cotton** adapts well to changing temperatures, is comfortable, and fire-resistant and protects against dust, abrasions and rough and irritating surfaces.

- **Duck** is a closely woven cotton fabric that protects against cuts and bruises when handling heavy, sharp or rough materials.

- **Leather** is often used to protect against dry heat and flames.

- **Rubber, rubberized fabrics, neoprene and plastics** protect against certain chemicals and physical hazards. When chemical or physical hazards are present, check with the clothing manufacturer to ensure that the material selected will provide protection against the specific hazard.

Hearing Protection

Determining the need to provide hearing protection for employees can be challenging. Employee exposure to excessive noise depends upon a number of factors, including:

- The loudness of the noise as measured in decibels (dB).

- The duration of each employee's exposure to the noise.

- Whether employees move between work areas with different noise levels.

▪ Whether noise is generated from one or multiple sources.

Generally, the louder the noise, the shorter the exposure time before hearing protection is required. For instance, employees may be exposed to a noise level of 90 dB for 8 hours per day (unless they experience a Standard Threshold Shift) before hearing protection is required. On the other hand, if the noise level reaches 115 dB hearing protection is required if the anticipated exposure exceeds 15 minutes.

For a more detailed discussion of the requirements for a comprehensive hearing conservation program, see OSHA Publication 3074 (2002), "Hearing Conservation" or refer to the OSHA standard at 29 CFR 1910.95, Occupational Noise Exposure, section (c).

Table 5, below, shows the permissible noise exposures that require hearing protection for employees exposed to occupational noise at specific decibel levels for specific time periods. Noises are considered continuous if the interval between occurrences of the maximum noise level is one second or less. Noises not meeting this definition are considered impact or impulse noises (loud momentary explosions of sound) and exposures to this type of noise must not exceed 140 dB. Examples of situations or tools that may result in impact or impulse noises are powder-actuated nail guns, a punch press or drop hammers.

Table 5
Permissible Noise Exposures

Duration per day, in hours	Sound level in dB*
8	90
6	92
4	95
3	97
2	100
1 1/2	102
1	105
1/2	110
1/4 or less	115

*When measured on the A scale of a standard sound level meter at slow response.
Source: 29 CFR 1910.95, Table G-16.

If engineering and work practice controls do not lower employee exposure to workplace noise to acceptable levels, employees must wear appropriate hearing protection. It is important to understand that hearing protectors reduce only the amount of noise that gets through to the ears. The amount of this reduction is referred to as attenuation, which differs according to the type of hearing protection used and how well it fits. Hearing protectors worn by employees must reduce an employee's noise exposure to within the acceptable limits noted in Table 5. Refer to Appendix B of 29 CFR 1910.95, Occupational Noise Exposure, for detailed information on methods to estimate the attenuation effectiveness of hearing protectors based on the device's noise reduction rating (NRR). Manufacturers of hearing protection devices must display the device's NRR on the product packaging. If employees are exposed to occupational noise at or above 85 dB averaged over an eight-hour period, the employer is required to institute a hearing conservation program that includes regular testing of employees' hearing by qualified professionals. Refer to 29 CFR 1910.95(c) for a description of the requirements for a hearing conservation program.

Some types of hearing protection include:

- **Single-use earplugs** are made of waxed cotton, foam, silicone rubber or fiberglass wool. They are self-forming and, when properly inserted, they work as well as most molded earplugs.

- **Pre-formed or molded earplugs** must be individually fitted by a professional and can be disposable or reusable. Reusable plugs should be cleaned after each use.

- **Earmuffs** require a perfect seal around the ear. Glasses, facial hair, long hair or facial movements such as chewing may reduce the protective value of earmuffs.

OSHA Assistance

OSHA can provide extensive help through a variety of programs, including technical assistance about effective safety and health programs, state plans, workplace consultations, voluntary protection programs, strategic partnerships, training and education, and more. An overall commitment to workplace safety and health can add value to your business, to your workplace and to your life.

Safety and Health Program Management Guidelines

Effective management of worker safety and health protection is a decisive factor in reducing the extent and severity of work-related injuries and illnesses and their related costs. In fact, an effective safety and health program forms the basis of good worker protection and can save time and money (about $4 for every dollar spent) and increase productivity and reduce worker injuries, illnesses and related workers' compensation costs.

To assist employers and employees in developing effective safety and health programs, OSHA published recommended Safety and Health Program Management Guidelines (Federal Register 54 (16): 3904-3916, January 26, 1989). These voluntary guidelines apply to all places of employment covered by OSHA.

The guidelines identify four general elements critical to the development of a successful safety and health management program:

- Management leadership and employee involvement.
- Work analysis.
- Hazard prevention and control.
- Safety and health training.

The guidelines recommend specific actions, under each of these general elements, to achieve an effective safety and health program. The Federal Register notice is available online at www.osha.gov.

State Programs

The Occupational Safety and Health Act of 1970 (OSH Act) encourages states to develop and operate their own job safety and health plans. OSHA approves and monitors these plans. There are currently 26 state plans: 23 cover both private and public (state and local government) employment; 3 states, Connecticut, New Jersey and New York, cover the public sector only. States and territories with their own OSHA-approved occupational safety and health plans must adopt standards identical to, or at least as effective as, the federal standards.

Consultation Services

Consultation assistance is available on request to employers who want help in establishing and maintaining a safe and healthful workplace. Largely funded by OSHA, the service is provided at no cost to the employer. Primarily developed for smaller employers with more hazardous operations, the consultation service is delivered by state governments employing professional safety and health consultants. Comprehensive assistance includes an appraisal of all-mechanical systems, work practices and occupational safety and health hazards of the workplace and all aspects of the employer's present job safety and health program. In addition, the service offers assistance to employers in developing and implementing an effective safety and health program. No penalties are proposed or citations issued for hazards identified by the consultant. OSHA provides consultation assistance to the employer with the assurance that his or her name and firm and any information about the workplace will not be routinely reported to OSHA enforcement staff.

Under the consultation program, certain exemplary employers may request participation in OSHA's Safety and Health Achievement Recognition Program (SHARP). Eligibility for participation in SHARP includes receiving a comprehensive consultation visit, demonstrating exemplary achievements in workplace safety and health by abating all identified hazards and developing an excellent safety and health program.

Employers accepted into SHARP may receive an exemption from programmed inspections (not complaint or accident investigation inspections) for a period of one year. For more information concerning consultation assistance, see the OSHA website at www.osha.gov.

Voluntary Protection Programs (VPP)

Voluntary Protection Programs and onsite consultation services, when coupled with an effective enforcement program, expand worker protection to help meet the goals of the OSH Act. The three levels of VPP are Star, Merit, and Demonstration designed to recognize outstanding achievements by companies that have successfully incorporated comprehensive safety and health programs into their total management system. The VPPs motivate others to achieve excellent safety and health results in the same outstanding way as they establish a cooperative relationship between employers, employees and OSHA.

For additional information on VPP and how to apply, contact the OSHA regional offices listed at the end of this publication.

Strategic Partnership Program

OSHA's Strategic Partnership Program, the newest member of OSHA's cooperative programs, helps encourage, assist and recognize the efforts of partners to eliminate serious workplace hazards and achieve a high level of worker safety and health. Whereas OSHA's Consultation Program and VPP entail one-on-one relationships between OSHA and individual worksites, most strategic partnerships seek to have a broader impact by building cooperative relationships with groups of employers and employees. These partnerships are voluntary, cooperative relationships between OSHA, employers, employee representatives and others (e.g., trade unions, trade and professional associations, universities and other government agencies).

For more information on this and other cooperative programs, contact your nearest OSHA office, or visit OSHA's website at www.osha.gov.

Alliance Programs

The Alliance Program enables organizations committed to workplace safety and health to collaborate with OSHA to prevent injuries and illnesses in the workplace. OSHA and the Alliance participants work together to reach out to, educate and lead the nation's employers and their employees in improving and advancing workplace safety and health.

Alliances are open to all groups, including trade or professional organizations, businesses, labor organizations, educational institutions and government agencies. In some cases, organizations may be building on existing relationships with OSHA that were developed through other cooperative programs.

There are few formal program requirements for Alliances and the agreements do not include an enforcement component. However, OSHA and the participating organizations must define, implement and meet a set of short- and long-term goals that fall into three categories: training and education; outreach and communication; and promoting the national dialogue on workplace safety and health.

OSHA Training and Education

OSHA area offices offer a variety of information services, such as compliance assistance, technical advice, publications, audiovisual aids and speakers for special engagements. OSHA's Training Institute in Arlington Heights, Ill., provides basic and advanced courses in safety and health for federal and state compliance officers, state consultants, federal agency personnel, and private sector employers, employees and their representatives.

The OSHA Training Institute also has established OSHA Training Institute Education Centers to address the increased demand for its courses from the private sector and from other federal agencies. These centers are nonprofit colleges, universities and other organizations that have been selected after a competition for participation in the program.

OSHA also provides funds to nonprofit organizations, through grants, to conduct workplace training and education in subjects where OSHA believes there is a lack of workplace training. Grants are awarded annually. Grant recipients are expected to contribute 20 percent of the total grant cost.

For more information on grants, training and education, contact the OSHA Training Institute, Office of Training and Education, 2020 South Arlington Heights Road, Arlington Heights, IL 60005, (847) 297-4810 or see "Outreach" on OSHA's website at www.osha.gov. For further information on any OSHA program, contact your nearest OSHA area or regional office listed at the end of this publication.

Information Available Electronically

OSHA has a variety of materials and tools available on its website at www.osha.gov. These include e-Tools such as Expert Advisors, Electronic Compliance Assistance Tools (e-cats), Technical Links; regulations, directives and publications, videos and other information for employers and employees. OSHA's software programs and compliance assistance tools walk you through challenging safety and health issues and common problems to find the best solutions for your workplace.

OSHA's CD-ROM includes standards, interpretations, directives and more, and can be purchased on CD-ROM from the U.S. Government Printing Office. To order, write to the Superintendent of Documents, P.O. Box 371954, Pittsburgh, PA 15250-7954 or phone (202) 512-1800, or order online at http://bookstore.gpo.gov.

OSHA Publications

OSHA has an extensive publications program. For a listing of free or sales items, visit OSHA's website at www.osha.gov or contact the OSHA Publications Office, U.S. Department of Labor, 200 Constitution Avenue, NW, N-3101, Washington, DC 20210. Telephone (202) 693-1888 or fax to (202) 693-2498.

Contacting OSHA

To report an emergency, file a complaint or seek OSHA advice, assistance or products, call (800) 321-OSHA or contact your nearest OSHA regional or area office listed at the end of this publication. The teletypewriter (TTY) number is (877) 889-5627.

You can also file a complaint online and obtain more information on OSHA federal and state programs by visiting OSHA's website at www.osha.gov.

OSHA Regional Offices

Region I
(CT,* ME, MA, NH, RI, VT*)
JFK Federal Building, Room E340
Boston, MA 02203
(617) 565-9860

Region II
(NJ,* NY,* PR,* VI*)
201 Varick Street, Room 670
New York, NY 10014
(212) 337-2378

Region III
(DE, DC, MD,* PA,* VA,* WV)
The Curtis Center
170 S. Independence Mall West
Suite 740 West
Philadelphia, PA 19106-3309
(215) 861-4900

Region IV
(AL, FL, GA, KY,* MS, NC,* SC,* TN*)
61 Forsyth Street, SW
Atlanta, GA 30303
(404) 562-2300

Region V
(IL, IN,* MI,* MN,* OH, WI)
230 South Dearborn Street, Room 3244
Chicago, IL 60604
(312) 353-2220

Region VI
(AR, LA, NM,* OK, TX)
525 Griffin Street, Room 602
Dallas, TX 75202
(214) 767-4731 or 4736 x224

Region VII
(IA,* KS, MO, NE)
City Center Square
1100 Main Street, Suite 800
Kansas City, MO 64105
(816) 426-5861

Region VIII
(CO, MT, ND, SD, UT,* WY*)
1999 Broadway, Suite 1690
PO Box 46550
Denver, CO 80201-6550
(303) 844-1600

Region IX
(American Samoa, AZ,* CA,* HI, NV,* Northern Mariana Islands)
71 Stevenson Street, Room 420
San Francisco, CA 94105
(415) 975-4310

Region X
(AK,* ID, OR,* WA*)
1111 Third Avenue, Suite 715
Seattle, WA 98101-3212
(206) 553-5930

*These states and territories operate their own OSHA-approved job safety and health programs (Connecticut, New Jersey and New York plans cover public employees only). States with approved programs must have a standard that is identical to, or at least as effective as, the federal standard.

Note: To get contact information for OSHA Area Offices, OSHA-approved State Plans and OSHA Consultation Projects, please visit us online at www.osha.gov or call us at 1-800-321-OSHA.

Appendix A
OSHA Standards that Require PPE

Standards that Require the Employer to Provide PPE:

1910.28	Safety requirements for scaffolds
1910.66	Powered platforms for building maintenance
1910.67	Vehicle-mounted elevating and rotating work platforms
1910.94	Ventilation
1910.119	Process safety management of highly hazardous chemicals
1910.120	Hazardous waste operations and emergency response
1910.132	General requirements (personal protective equipment)
1910.133	Eye and face protection
1910.135	Occupational foot protection
1910.136	Occupational foot protection
1910.137	Electrical protective devices
1910.138	Hand protection
1910.139	Respiratory protection for M. tuberculosis
1910.157	Portable fire extinguishers
1910.160	Fixed extinguishing systems, general
1910.183	Helicopters
1910.218	Forging machines
1910.242	Hand and portable powered tools and equipment, general
1910.243	Guarding of portable power tools
1910.252	General requirements (welding, cutting and brazing)
1910.261	Pulp, paper, and paperboard mills
1910.262	Textiles
1910.268	Telecommunications
1910.269	Electric power generation, transmission and distribution
1910.333	Selection and use of work practices
1910.335	Safeguards for personnel protection
1910.1000	Air contaminants
1910.1003	13 carcinogens, etc.
1910.1017	Vinyl chloride
1910.1029	Coke oven emissions
1910.1043	Cotton dust
1910.1096	Ionizing radiation

Standards that Require the Employer to Provide PPE
at No Cost to the Employee:

1910.95	Occupational noise exposure
1910.134	Respiratory protection
1910.146	Permit-required confined spaces
1910.156	Fire brigades
1910.266	Logging operations
1910.1001	Asbestos
1910.1018	Inorganic Arsenic
1910.1025	Lead
1910.1027	Cadmium
1910.1028	Benzene
1910.1030	Bloodborne pathogens
1910.1044	1,2-dibromo-3-chloropropane
1910.1045	Acrylonitrile
1910.1047	Ethylene oxide
1910.1048	Formaldehyde
1910.1050	Methylenedianiline
1910.1051	1,3-Butadiene
1910.1052	Methylene chloride
1910.1450	Occupational exposure to chemicals in laboratories

29 CFR 1915, Shipyard Employment
Standards that Require the Employer to Provide PPE:

1915.12	Precautions and the order of testing before entering confined and enclosed spaces and other dangerous atmospheres
1915.13	Cleaning and other cold work
1915.32	Toxic cleaning solvents
1915.34	Mechanical paint removers
1915.35	Painting
1915.51	Ventilation and protection in welding, cutting and heating
1915.73	Guarding of deck openings and edges
1915.77	Working surfaces
1915.135	Powder actuated fastening tools
1915.156	Foot protection
1915.157	Hand and body protection
1915.158	Lifesaving equipment
1915.159	Personal fall arrest systems (PFAS)

Standards that Require the Employer to Provide PPE at No Cost to the Employee:

1915.154	Respiratory Protection
1915.1001	Asbestos

29 CFR 1917, Marine Terminals
Standards that Require the Employer to Provide PPE:

1917.22	Hazardous cargo
1917.25	Fumigants, pesticides, insecticides and hazardous waste
1917.26	First aid and lifesaving facilities
1917.91	Eye and face protection
1917.93	Head protection
1917.95	Other protective measures
1917.126	River banks
1917.152	Welding, cutting and heating (hot work)
1917.154	Compressed air

Standards that Require the Employer to Provide PPE at No Cost to the Employee:

1917.92	Respiratory protection

29 CFR 1918, Longshoring
Standards that Require the Employer to Provide PPE:

1918.85	Containerized cargo operations
1918.88	Log operations
1918.93	Hazardous atmospheres and substances
1918.94	Ventilation and atmospheric conditions
1918.104	Foot protection
1918.105	Other protective measures

Standards that Require the Employer to Provide PPE at No Cost to the Employee:

1918.102	Respiratory protection

29 CFR 1926, Construction
Standards that Require the Employer to Provide PPE:

1926.28	Personal protective equipment
1926.52	Occupational noise exposure

1926.57	Ventilation
1926.64	Process safety management of highly hazardous chemicals
1926.65	Hazardous waste operations and emergency response
1926.95	Criteria for personal protective equipment
1926.96	Occupational foot protection
1926.100	Head protection
1926.101	Hearing protection
1926.102	Eye and face protection
1926.104	Safety belts, lifelines and lanyards
1926.105	Safety nets
1926.106	Working over or near water
1926.250	General requirements for storage
1926.300	General requirements (Hand and power tools)
1926.302	Power-operated hand tools
1926.304	Woodworking tools
1926.353	Ventilation and protection in welding, cutting and heating
1926.354	Welding, cutting and heating in way of preservative coatings
1926.416	General requirements (Electrical)
1926.451	General requirements (Scaffolds)
1926.453	Aerial lifts
1926.501	Duty to have fall protection
1926.502	Fall protection systems criteria and practices
1926.550	Cranes and derricks
1926.551	Helicopters
1926.701	General requirements (Concrete and masonry construction)
1926.760	Fall protection (Steel erection)
1926.800	Underground construction
1926.951	Tools and protective equipment
1926.955	Overhead lines
1926.1101	Asbestos

Standards that Require the Employer to Provide PPE at No Cost to the Employee:

1926.60	Methylenedianiline
1926.62	Lead
1926.103	Respiratory protection
1926.1127	Cadmium